# THE NOT-FOR-PROFIT CEO
# A SURVIVOR'S MANUAL

by
George B. Wright

**C3 Publications**
Portland, Oregon

Copyright © 1992 by George B. Wright
All rights reserved
including the right of reproduction
in whole or in part in any form.
Published by C3 Publications
A division of C3 Strategies
3495 NW Thurman
Portland, OR 97210-1283
First Edition

Library of Congress Catalogue Card Number 92-81341
ISBN 0-9632655-0-4

Book designed by: Melissa Melgreen
Cover design by: Dan Fast

Printed in the United States of America

Dedicated to those men and women who have committed their professional lives to guiding the soul of voluntarism.

# Table of Contents

# INTRODUCTION

# The Not-For-Profit CEO
# A Survivor's Manual

In over 25 years as a professional in the not-for-profit (NFP) sector, I have identified six basic elements of management survival which have worked for me. Frankly, I discovered most of them by making my share of mistakes along the way. And while these techniques are not new or revolutionary, I've never seen them put down succinctly; ready to use, free of theory and academic double-speak, and in less than 300 pages. These six "checkpoints" may apply most directly to the CEO, however I found them to be key at every level as my career moved forward. So, whether you're already the Chief Executive Officer, you want to be, or you're a board member wondering what it's like to manage a NFP organization — listen up! We're going to cover a lot of ground in short order.

**Get out your yellow high-lighter and slash over any "bell ringers" we pass.** Then, when you've read the book through, **read it again**. Make this your personal guide. It isn't a sacred tome, make notes in the margins, use a high-lighter;

*Notes*

whatever works for you. Refer to it whenever you run into a question or problem related to any of the key elements we will cover. Most problems and challenges you'll encounter as a CEO will fall within the range of these components. We'll cover some methods to solve daily problems and help you develop, or revisit, your skills for the long term. Not surprisingly, these techniques will not only help you survive your job, they will be good for your organization as well. Let's face it, most of your management skills are learned in the saddle; by doing.

So, let's do it. Together, we'll examine the **six checkpoints** of managing successfully in the not-for-profit environment. But first, I'll ask you to pass muster on **four assumptions** about the soundness of your organization. Once those are resolved, we'll take on the real issues and answers to empower your own success as a NFP CEO.

George B. Wright

# PREFACE

# Assumptions

Before we get into the nitty-gritty, let's take a few minutes to get some things straight. Managing a not-for-profit corporation is a challenging and satisfying experience — **if** you can respond positively to **four basic assumptions**. Check them out. Can you answer in the affirmative to the following assumptions? If not, you need to do some serious evaluation. I urge you to read the following very carefully before proceeding further:

➤ **Assumption #1:** Your organization has a board of directors which recognizes you and the position of CEO (Executive Director, Executive Vice President, Managing Director, President or other title), and empowers you with the authority and respect to do your job. By the way, some feel it is an arrogant assumption, or commercialization of the NFP environment, to call NFP administrators CEOs. I disagree. I think it is merely an outgrowth of the maturation of the sector. That may be positive or disappointing, but change drives all processes. But what your title is, is less important that what it

*Notes*

means and how you and your position are considered.

➤ **Assumption #2:** Your organization is at least reasonably well organized, *i.e.,* incorporated, has formal bylaws, meets all local, state and federal guidelines, is fiscally accountable to the public and its members, provides its board with liability insurance, bonds its staff, and has credible policies and benefits for its employees.

➤ **Assumption #3:** Your organization is in at least fair financial condition, *i.e.,* not filing for bankruptcy, is meeting its financial obligations (paying the rent, phone bill, heat, etc.), meeting payroll and has at the minimum a moderately dependable source of income, as well as a board which accepts its responsibility for helping generate financial support.

➤ **Assumption #4:** Your organization is free of political intrigue and treachery, *i.e.,* no staff trying to sabotage the CEO, no board members playing power politics or abusing the conflict of interest policy, nor a CEO mistreating staff or managing through intimidation, and a board which makes it clear that such tactics will not be tolerated.

If any of the above assumptions is not true, your organization is likely in need of immediate remedial care. Disaster management is not the theme of this volume. If indeed your organization does not meet all of these assumptions, that fact must be addressed at once; for they each represent major organizational requirements. It will be impossible for any CEO to be truly effective if even one of these bench marks is flawed. *Seek professional advice and counsel appropriate to the specific deficiencies.* And if you're the problem, I hope you can recognize that and do something about it; if not, your board may do something about it for you.

I'm not saying an organization has to be perfect in every way, just free of fatal flaws. Besides, the perfect voluntary organization wouldn't need a seasoned CEO, or any staff. Virtually all not-for-profit organizations (NFPO) began without staff. But you needn't worry, an organization large enough to support management, needs management. And that means you.

So, if your organization generally meets our list of assumptions, and carries the usual list of imperfections, you are in a position to manage. Let's see if we can help you survive the challenge, and thrive.

# CHECKPOINT ONE

# Managing a Democracy

The not-for-profit (NFP) culture is broken out in a very specific triad: the board which hired you, the corps of volunteers who work with you, and the staff who work for and with you. Each is separate and distinct, yet diffuse and interrelated. Never forget that. Let me say that again. Each segment of the triad has its own purpose and personality, and yet all three are part of the organizational fabric; interconnected.

Should you overlook that fact of life, you could be wondering what happened to your career. But you're the boss, right? It's not that simple. You are a diplomat, an ombudsman, and a steward who must manage decisively and lead dynamically while never disrupting the triad. Never forget that each segment of the triad has a constituency among one or more of the other two segments.

For example, executive director Mary has a staff member, Ralph, who has been speaking to volunteers in opposition of a new program which has been authorized by the board. Mary is getting feedback from volunteers and staff regarding

*Notes*

13

Ralph's actions. She confronts Ralph and reminds him that the program is authorized and will go forward. Ralph restates his opposition to Mary, who says that she understands the complaint, but instructs Ralph to move ahead. But soon after, more reports flow back to Mary that Ralph persists in his negative resistance. Again Mary confronts Ralph, who still opposes the program and lets it be known that he has also spoken with a board member and convinced him that the program is a bad idea.

There are several ways this problem could be resolved, but the point here is to **never act without first considering the triad**. How will a given action taken with one segment impact the other two? Should Mary reprimand or perhaps fire Ralph? That is not even the question at this point. The question is, is Mary ready to act? No. Not unless she has judged how any disciplinary action taken with Ralph will affect the three components of the organization. And here, we're assuming Mary would use prudent management technique; seek the advice of her human resources committee, or other such professional resource, and work for a positive resolution. But even that is not enough. The human resources committee will cover legal, regulatory and procedural concerns. It will not tell you how a certain board member, or the staff, will react to the abrupt dismissal of Ralph when they may even be in agreement with him. In fact, they don't even have to care about the issue itself. Maybe they just like Ralph. He's the staff person who works with their committee, or is part of their staff team, or he merely hits it off with a certain board member.

See how it works? Never, I repeat, never take potentially controversial action carelessly just because you're the CEO or know you're in the right. Always sleep on it. Close your office door, take out a note pad and consider the triad. **And remember these three things:**

**1)** Your board acts as a unit and must be considered whenever any management action may disrupt the triad regardless of your authority. The board should back your management decisions, but individually they are also volunteers and will move to another part of the triad; they merge.

**2)** Volunteers generally are involved in an organization because they want to do good, enjoy themselves and be around people they like. But never underestimate the influence of volunteers whose ire has been raised because they feel that as CEO, you have acted improperly; particularly on people issues.

**3)** Your staff works for you as CEO, but they will also develop close bonds among the volunteers with whom they work on a regular basis. It makes no difference how well or poorly staff does their jobs (unless there is blatant incompetence), the volunteers will bond with them and go to bat for them. Ironically, you want this kind of support of your staff, but don't forget that it exists when you have to take action with an employee.

So you see, you not only work for the board, but for the volunteers and, yes, even for your staff. The irony of managing the not-for-profit is that to use the full power of your authority, you have to give much of it up. The true power of your influence is in considering all three segments of the triad when important issues call for action, and then marshalling support with skill and purpose. You must assess the problem, determine the players and select a course of action. Before exercising your authority over any controversial issue, always decide which of your in-house constituencies needs to be informed, convinced of your plan of action, or even brought into the actual resolution process.

Let's get back to Mary. In the incident with Ralph, she is faced with one of the most potentially damaging dilemmas a NFP CEO can face, the severe disciplinary action or firing of an employee. No matter how glaring Ralph's insubordination may be, Mary must manage her democracy thoughtfully on this issue. Being right isn't enough. In this case, Mary should apprise her president of the problem and relate that she is working on a solution. The president should accept the information, but not interfere with the management process. Thus informed, the president will be prepared if another volunteer, or even Ralph, makes contact.

Next, Mary should meet with the committee chair, the person who works most closely with Ralph on the issue in question. She should explain the situation and that as CEO she will be taking responsible, thoughtful action. She should also let the chairperson know that she has conferred with the board president. Any advice offered by the volunteer should be accepted politely, but in no instance should Mary even hint that she is accepting direction from volunteers on personnel decisions. Of course, we must assume that Mary is consulting with her human resources committee for professional advice. But the final decision regarding Ralph must come from Mary.

## RECAP

 All not-for-profits operate from a triad: board, volunteer corps, and staff. The effective CEO enhances the management of this culture by thoroughly understanding and managing the elements of the triad. It should become second nature. When issues of controversy arise, the CEO must react with practiced skill; patient, insightful, aware of how each segment of the triad affects the other. Effective use of the triad, however, should be ongoing and is not only for resolving controversy. In fact, properly understood and administered, it supports a three-legged management stool which can help maintain a healthy organization, which in turn makes for an equally healthy CEO.

# CHECKPOINT TWO

# Search & Deploy

Your job as CEO of a not-for-profit-organization is complex, certainly requiring more skill than may be understood by the very board which hired you. I have already alluded to some of the varied talents you must possess and use proficiently to do your job well. Add this one to the list: **recruiter**.

It is difficult to declare one trait more essential than any others to be a successful NFP CEO. But if I had to choose one, it would be recruiting. You and your organization can only be as strong as the people who align themselves with your mission. Talent and clout do not fall like manna from the skies. In fact, it is just the opposite. Competition for the best and brightest, be it volunteers or staff, is intense. There are several reasons for that. For example, women have moved into the work place in ever increasing numbers over the past two decades. The result is that a once abundant source of willing volunteer workers, the American housewife, has literally vanished. What remains is a diminishing rank of older female volunteers, from an era when they belonged to long standing organiza-

*Notes*

tions which encouraged, even insisted, on community service from their members. Those organizations are fading away and today most women no longer identify with them.

Next, our population is aging rapidly. It would seem that with a growing pool of healthy and able retirees that our not-for-profit organizations would be overflowing with willing senior volunteers. Not so. First the former organizational networks no longer link up in this new era of retired American. In addition, our older citizens are less liberal with their disposable time. And when they do volunteer, they want to serve in a meaningful role. Most of them have worked, men and women, and should be respected for their professional expertise. Today's older volunteers must be recruited through a different set of networks, everything from the associations of retired professionals to major companies which maintain internal organizations for former employees.

All of that said, how much time should the CEO personally devote to recruiting retired volunteers? None. Zero. Turn that responsibility over to other staff, or trained volunteers. Why? Because as important as those volunteers can be to your organization, you need to concentrate your time elsewhere. The only exception would be selected high level retired professionals, *i.e.*, former corporate leaders, administrators of academic institutions, medical centers or government agencies. In other words, retired clout, retained influence. In those instances, the CEO should definitely be involved.

Let me make another point here. About competition. Every other NFPO in your community is after the same talent, influence and expertise that you want. If their mousetrap is better than yours, they will beat you. You will lose the cream and be left with the skim. Maybe not bad, just not great. You can't build great organizations on mediocre talent. For that reason every person in your organization, board member, staff and volunteer, as well as you, should be a recruiter. I also firmly believe that the CEO should be the one to close the deal with all new volunteers; with the exception of hands-on office level volunteers or very large NFPOs. What you want from the board and staff are referrals. Names of people who might be potential volunteers. Key point. Let it be known that you want to personally meet and interview every referral. Why?

Here is the essence of why. I believe that strategically, the task most critical to your professional success is *top recruiter*. As CEO, you are subject to evaluation, formal and informal. Part of that process focuses on such clear issues as budget, generation of revenue, and delivery of services. Obvious stuff, right? Often less obvious is that all evaluation is really based on the quality of the people you've drawn into the organization.

Next key point. As your organization's chief recruiter, you walk another one of those thin lines. You can mold the clay, but you can't be the one to put it into the firing oven. In other words, you do the research, the screening interviews, the introductory orientation, and most importantly, the assessment of where best to use a specific person's talents, or if to use them at all. You do everything but provide the final stamp of approval. That you must reserve for the volunteers. The nominating committee should recommend volunteers to the president for appointment to committees, or nominations to the board for new directors and officers. You search, recruit, screen, recommend and serve as an important resource. But once the nominating committee, the president or the board convene to finalize the selection process, you must step back.

But earlier didn't I say the CEO should be the closer with each new volunteer? Yes. Didn't I just contradict that? No. Let me be frank. By the time you go to the nominating committee, or the president, you are presenting winners. You have people who have been screened, given the organization's story, who have bought into your mission, agreed to serve in some specific manner and are ready to be anointed. Face it, you are the closer. The volunteers will respect your recommendations and willingly take them into the fold, if you do your job well, honestly and objectively.

Is it appropriate for the CEO to do all of that? Shouldn't the volunteers do most of the screening and selection? I suppose there are some who would disagree with me, but absolutely not. The CEO knows better than anyone, or had better know, the human resource needs and weaknesses of his or her organization, whether at the board, committee or staff level. It is entirely appropriate, if not essential, that the CEO be a major cog in seeking out good board material, have input on officer nominees, and be the major scout for new talent. Certainly, and I reiterate, there is a protocol which demands that the CEO knows when he or she has reached the limit of his or her direct influence. When that limit has been reached, the volunteer leadership takes over. However, if the CEO has done the job well, his or her expectations will blend with those of the volunteers. During the process of recruitment and appointment, the CEO/volunteer partnership is at its highest level. The future of the organization is dependent upon both accepting their role and living up to it. It requires a mutual sense of trust and respect.

Okay, agreed it's vital that the CEO be the top gun when it comes to recruiting. Easier said than done? Maybe you don't like recruiting.

Maybe you disagree with me and think that it really is the volunteers' role. But think about it. If you aren't willing to overcome your dislike of recruiting, or you are adamant that only volunteers should lead the way, you are saying that you're willing to settle for an average talent base for your organization. That's right. Without your personal commitment and leadership, your organization will soon lose its competitive edge or forever attract average talent. No cutting edge for you. To grow in impact, resources and quality, your pool of talent must continually improve and change to meet future needs. Some of that will come through the maturation, training and on-the-job experience for current talent, but that will not be enough. Every organization needs to continually attract a new level of expertise and influence. In addition, every organization loses good people who burn out, move from the area or simply want a different volunteer challenge. Replenishment alone requires your attention.

Which is more important, to recruit a great staff or dynamic volunteers? The obvious answer is that you need both, that they feed off of each other. If I have any bias on this chicken or the egg question, it probably leans slightly in favor of staff, for one not so simple reason - facilitation. While you need comparative strengths from each, you have to use your volunteers effectively right from the beginning. This is dependent on a capable staff to facilitate those volunteer strengths. We'll get into *facilitation* in the next checkpoint. But for now let's start with the primary ingredients of recruiting:

# Volunteers

1) **Assess:** First and foremost, you must continually be assessing your base of volunteer talent, identifying gaps and weaknesses and confirming your strengths. You and you alone will see the entire picture. Staff or key volunteers will only be aware of their specific area of responsibility.

2) **Ongoing:** Recruitment has to be ongoing; never stop selling. There is a tendency in organizations to throw a nominating committee together for a couple of months once a year, just before the annual meeting or year-end. Keep your nominating

process in gear year-round. Be open to every opportunity to bring fresh blood into the organization. You will never have to worry about having too many good volunteers.

**3) Referral:** Force-feed a referral program among your board, staff and volunteers. Provide a mechanism (a simple form is enough), making it easy to submit potential volunteer candidates. Then, regularly encourage everyone in the organization to refer names throughout the year. Next, make it a personal policy to recognize those volunteers and staff who are actively recruiting. Mention their efforts in the organization's newsletter or in your own report to the board of directors.

**4) Screening:** The CEO should be the first point of contact with each potential board or committee level volunteer, for several reasons. It is a sign of respect that the CEO would make time to meet them. You can give them the best overview of the organization, you can screen out weak candidates or point them to duties less critical. You will be best able to help them focus on where they might want to devote their volunteer time, and finally, you can help those unsuited for your organization talk themselves out of volunteering. The CEO is really the only person in the organization who can effectively do all of those things. Yes, it does take time, but what better place to invest some of your time than in picking the best people for the right job.

**5) Assume Your Role:** The most important recruitment is for board members. Many times board candidates will come from among existing volunteers in the organization. In this case, your role with the nominating committee will be to help assess the strengths and weaknesses of these known people. It is entirely appropriate for you to do this, if not essential. If you know a volunteer to be a procrastinator who does not follow through, the nominating committee needs to know that. Don't worry, the committee will assume its authority when it officially sets the slate, a role from which you are excluded. But you should contribute diplomatically, even assertively, up to that point. If you maintain your own objectivity and high ethical standards, the committee members will respect your input and appreciate your insights.

When it comes to recruiting board talent new to the organization, you work for the nominating committee and the overall benefit of the organization. In most cases, the nominating committee will solicit nominees from the board, staff and volunteers, and do some of the search on their own. But the CEO must assert him or herself at this point as well. Once specific skills (legal, banking, media, marketing, etc.), or other criteria have been identified, the CEO should offer to conduct research and indentify a list of possible candidates for each board slot to be filled. It is important that this role not be denied you. You are the only one who will objectively seek strong new talent. Frankly, volunteers often tend to clone themselves, which holds back the growth of the board over time. This may not show up for awhile, but over the years the board will remain locked into the same range of horsepower, which in actuality is losing ground.

**6) Strategy:** Your recruitment strategy should be one which maximizes your personal influence, experience and networking resources. As the CEO you automatically bring the prestige of the organization with you. That alone will open doors not available to others. You can meet effectively with business leaders, presidents of institutions, and administrators of agencies. Of course you should always use the clout you already have on the nominating committee or board to open doors or provide valuable introductions. Use every tool available.

Once you have identified the skills, experience and influence you'll be seeking, and other criteria (such as multicultural representation), map out your research and recruitment strategy based on your experience and contacts. One method which has been used effectively is to meet with people who you are *not* seeking as candidates, but who possess position and influence. From them you will seek names of people known to them who might be excellent candidates and meet your criteria. However, keep criteria flexible or you may pass over some potentially exceptional prospects.

Once your influential contacts have provided you with names of possible candidates, ask them for an introduction. Usually they will oblige. You want them to help you break through any barriers busy people commonly put in place. And on occasion, one of those persons of influence whose advice you've sought will offer their own services. Bingo!

**7) Qualities:** One of the most important elements of recruiting, which you must remember as the CEO, is: *Don't be easy on yourself.* And right near the top of a list of board qualities is *challenge*. If a CEO only seeks people who will rubber stamp his actions, or join her fan club, such methods will undermine the ethical standards of the profession. You must be willing to recruit people who will challenge you and the organization. I'm not saying to recruit troublemakers. In fact, I think you should look for people who relate to you, who respect you and like you, but they must also have high expectations of you. The organization as a whole needs to hold its feet to the fire and that includes the CEO.

**8) Clout:** As I said earlier, competition in the NFP world is a reality. To survive and flourish, your organization needs to compete aggressively. This includes competing for volunteer talent as well as for dollars and public awareness. Without volunteer leaders who have some clout, the resources will be harder to get. It's a balancing act. You must recruit this influence without shattering the balance on your board. Bring on too much horsepower too soon and you won't keep them without peer to peer equity. Plus, you run the risk of insulting or demoralizing some existing members of your board. Also remember, all clout with no compassion for the mission is no good either. You need clout, just balance it with commitment.

**9) Real Tasks:** The biggest disservice to a volunteer is to recruit them and then have nothing meaningful for them to do. It's an insult to the person recruited, a waste of their talents, a risk to their potential commitment, and an embarrassment to you and the organization. And yet we've all done it. We can often be so intent on landing dynamic talent that we forget to plug them into some real work. Today's volunteers are very concerned with savoring their disposable time. They will contribute pieces of it to causes and organizations which fit their own agendas. If you appear disorganized, or you waste their time, they will simply move on. Not only have you lost them, they can harm your organization's reputation; and you run the risk of discouraging other potential volunteers or financial supporters from joining or contributing to the organization.

**10) Rewarding Environment:** Volunteers thrive in an environment which is positive; rewarding. They frequently come from their own pressure-packed work situations. A big part of the reason they volunteer is to serve with good people, for an important mission in a nurturing environment. As CEO, you must do everything possible to provide such an experience. It helps to look at each volunteer as a client or a guest. Your organization should be a place where they are always welcome and respected. After all, you recruited them, you owe them no less. That doesn't mean they shouldn't be expected to produce. It does cost organizational resources to support them. So they should live up to spe-

cific expectations, but in a caring re-
ceptive environment.

## Staff

Recruiting volunteers requires dil-
igence, empathy, a certain strategy
and selling. And it never stops. At
the staff level, you will attract people
with motives often similar to those
of your volunteers. The difference is
that usually they come to you. If you
run a healthy organization and have
a good reputation as CEO, you will
attract talented, quality applicants
for any job. Warning. Many people
who have never worked for a not-
for-profit will respond to your job
announcements, especially for posi-
tions in accounting, marketing,
computer technician and secretary;
all of the so-called cross-over jobs,
jobs that are not necessarily sector
specific.

Today, more than ever before,
people want to make a difference.
They want to work for a cause they
can support. Sometimes, it's easy to
become mesmerized by a charming,
bubbly applicant who is just dying
to work for your cause. Take your
time. Don't abandon your usual

good judgement. Also, look carefully at someone who is tired of working for *crass commericialism* and is willing to work for a reduced salary. Even if they are sincere, and most are, if the dollar cut is severely out of line, I guarantee you they will start thinking about that lost income from day one. They will either appeal to you for more money after all, making your life miserable, or leave in a few months.

You want talented, intelligent people; people whose experience and training fit your needs at the right price for both parties. Next, look for people who can fulfill specific job requirements *better than you;* maybe even take your job one day. And you want strong people skills. The successful NFP is in the people business first and foremost. Sour pusses, curt mannerisms and arrogance are out. I don't care how talented a person may be, if they can't relate positively to people, they won't function well in a NFPO.

Most NFPs run a tight ship, with small to moderate sized staffs and lean budgets. You want staff who work well together, are willing to help others, even if it's not their job or department. You want healthy self-esteem, not pompous egos. Even if you happen to run a large NFP, you likely don't have an over abundance of people at any position, so you need self-starters who work well independently.

A big order? Strong people skills, confident personalities, no big egos, team players, but people who also work well on their own? They're out there. And they want to work for you. Why? Because you offer a challenging environment where their talents will be used to the fullest. They're going to feel a sense of accomplishment, make a real contribution to society, and work in a positive setting with great people.

But alas, there is competition for this kind of talent too. Be as competitive with your salary structure as possible, offer the best benefits you can, budget for staff development, and be sure that your organization knows where it is going.

And, don't forget. Check those references before you hire.

# RECAP

**RECAP**

You should be the top gun when it comes to recruiting in your organization. Literally, the success of your administration depends on the quality of those around you. Turn over the recruitment and care and feeding of office level volunteers to a good staff member or qualified volunteers. The rest is yours, after this caveat: Know how to walk the thin line between your impact on recruiting and the protocol of final decision making by the volunteers. You are after the best volunteers available. You want talent, expertise and clout. To get that, you do the research, networking, initial up-front assessment, screening and the close on every candidate. Remember, when I say close, I mean everything that can possibly be completed before turning a candidate over to the volunteer process for final determination. Yes, it is appropriate for the CEO to be the prime mover in recruiting. He or she has the widest overall view and knowledge of the organization. But don't be easy on yourself,

do what is best for the organization. Recruit challengers.

# CHECKPOINT THREE

# Relate, Relate, Facilitate

Webster:  Fa-cil-i-tate, v., to make easier

*Notes*

One of the most challenging tasks for the paid staff of any not-for-profit is to facilitate. Volunteers were recruited to be used, not to be spectators. But so very often, accomplishments in the voluntary environment move slowly. Eager, talented staff will chafe to get on with it.

It is up to the CEO to constantly remind his or her staff to not get out in front of their volunteers. Or worse yet, staff can find it much easier to not involve volunteers at all. They just exclude them. And of course, there are some staff responsibilities which do not require volunteer input; that's why there is staff in the first place. The key is to separate those functions which are totally staff driven from those which call for volunteer participation.

However, once you've made those distinctions, don't play games with your volunteers—at any level. Once you have given a volunteer a specific assignment, you must honor that implied agreement; the agreement to utilize their talents, give them full partnership, provide appropriate resources, and live up to agreed dates and timetables. And never usurp the assumed responsibilities or authority of volunteers once set, unless they are blatantly neglecting their charge.

## The Volunteers Came First

Most commonly, in fact almost exclusively, not-for-profit-organizations are begun without paid staff and are initially driven by committed volunteers. This is an important point to be remembered. As essential as the staff may be to your organization today, there was probably a time when there were no hired hands. Your NFPO may have been run solely by volunteers for many years, or just during its developmental phase. None-the-less, a staff was hired to do what the volunteers could not or would not do alone, when the scale of things outstripped their available time, energy and resources.

As the sophistication of the NFP sector has increased, staff and volunteers work more as partners, each supporting the role of the other.

Most staffs today are comprised of professionals, often highly trained in their fields and able to work shoulder to shoulder with volunteers. Today's NFP CEO must administer his or her NFP corporation with skill equal to, if not surpassing, that of his or her counterpart in the for-profit sector.

Having said all of that, staff still must serve the volunteers. At the top of every staff member's list of responsibilities in the NFPO must be facilitating the volunteers under their charge. They should make things easier and more productive. Each volunteer is giving your organization a piece of their lives — willingly, donating precious hours taken from work, family, recreation and other pursuits.

When that person enters your building, under normal circumstances you may have one or two hours of their time. If you or your staff are doing your job, the volunteer should already know what is going to happen, be ready to contribute, invest in the meeting or activity, then sign off on an assignment and commit to the next such meeting or activity. You are, after all, managing a voluntary organization. Essential to that culture is the art of facilitation:

**1) Agendas Are Covenants:** Like it or not, NFPOs function through groups of people, who agree to get together and do something. These groups are usually called committees. Committees are the brunt of countless jokes, moans and groans. Some consultants to organizations even suggest getting rid of them — to use task forces instead. What is a task force? A group of people meeting *temporarily*. Ah, a short-term committee. Whatever the title, in each case, we have a group of people meeting to deal with specific responsibilities.

We'll leave it to you as to whether you primarily use committees, task forces, or something else altogether. Most committees are probably task forces that didn't want to quit, or lost sight of their objective, which has since been lost to antiquity. But one simple fact is true for each group — they need help to stay focused.

The best tool for an effective volunteer/staff team is the agenda. Properly used, the agenda creates productive unity between staff and the volunteers with whom they work. The problem is, agendas are one of the most abused, least well used tools in most NFPOs.

Properly used, the agenda makes heroes of everybody. The committee chair becomes an effective leader, the professional staff member is respected by the chair, and the committee members feel productive and confident in both the chair and staff. So, if agendas are so great, why aren't they used effectively? Truly, I think it is because they are considered a mere necessity, a trivial duty. Actually, agendas deserve a lofty priority.

In fact, an agenda is a covenant between chair and staff, and a promise to committee members, who are the most vulnerable in this relationship. The staff member assigned to the committee is the facilitator. He or she works with the chair prior to each meeting. Together they determine what needs to happen at the coming meeting. They map out a course of action, prioritize the issues to be dealt with, and put it all down in writing. Presto, an agenda. If all of this sounds elementary, maybe it's because you're taking it too lightly. Think about what these two people have done.

Together, they have created a covenant: *a formal, binding agreement*, according to our friend Webster. This agreement guarantees the committee that they will meet on a specific date, at a certain hour, for a set amount of time, and conduct specific business. To be more direct, you've agreed to not waste their time and to accomplish something.

The agenda is one of the ultimate tools of facilitation, bonding staff and volunteers to a common purpose. Properly administered, the "agenda process" enhances the confidence of everyone involved in the credibility of the organization and the reputation of its staff. In addition, it makes winners of the volunteers. That is what facilitating is all about, creating winners.

**2) The Board and its Leaders:** As CEO, you are also a facilitator. A prime function of the organization's administrator is to facilitate the board, its president, its officers, its directors and its process. In other words, all of these people had better feel focused, respected, informed, safe, effective and look good doing it. For instance, your board president should be briefed on every important or potentially thorny issue known to you and your staff. Do not under any circumstances embarrass your president, never. Keep that person informed.

If there is bad news, the next phone call you make is to your president. (Of course I'm speaking here of important issues, not ticky-tacky office problems) If there is even a remote chance that the media might contact your president — get there first. Be sure he or she is conversant on the subject in question, or at least can handle the issue intelligently; even if that means no comment. By the same token, be sure your president and other leaders get a piece of the media limelight whenever it occurs, not just you or your staff.

I suggest that you meet regularly with your board president; weekly, biweekly, monthly - whatever works for you. Get close to that person. Share with them and network, each helping the other. The president is almost as vulnerable as the CEO in some ways; alone at the top, subject to criticism by his or her peers and afraid of embarrassment or making critical errors in judgement. Hopefully, this person is someone you can trust to confidentiality because you may need to speak frankly with them on occasion. By all means, find a way to make your president a winner. I always asked my incoming president what they wanted most to accomplish during their term. We found a way for them to leave some sort of positive legacy behind them.

Don't forget the covenant, the agenda you and your president craft for the board meetings. Put a lot of thought and planning into it. The issues brought to the board should be clear, focused and of importance. Get rid of as much trivia as possible. At this level don't waste people's time.

Also do not forget the other officers on your board: treasurer, secretary, vice-president and president elect. Show respect for their roles. You want them to be focused as effective board members, helping to make critical decisions. If they don't feel valued in their posts, they won't be fully in tune and could even become troublesome and disgruntled.

Finally, as chief facilitator, you can be a major catalyst in helping the board remain focused on the mission and purpose of the organization, as opposed to the color of the new carpet or which brand of computer to buy. Perhaps a delicate task at times, but one of great importance which you and your president must keep before you.

**3) Committees and Chairs:** As the CEO, you are the caretaker of your organization's culture of voluntarism. You are the steward of the *volunteers' bill of rights*. You are also the primary role model and lead facilitator to your staff. Right after recruitment, the act of facilitating is next on your management hit list. Once you've got 'em, use 'em. Your staff must buy into their responsibilities here, and position themselves appropriately in relationship to the volunteers. There is a definite professional etiquette which staff must recognize and practice.

Since most major organizational achievements pass through committees, it is critical that you and your staff pay close attention to your committees and their chairs. Relate, relate, facilitate! Remember what I said earlier? Agendas are covenants. They are also important in helping assigned staff actually facilitate their professional responsibilities.

Now here's an, Aha! *The agenda gives the staff power when dealing with the chairs of committees.* Professional etiquette dictates that staff shall facilitate; lead without really *leading*, guide while *yielding* to a chairperson's authority over committee process. Of course, the first thing the staff member should do is establish a rapport with the committee chair. Meet with them immediately after they've been appointed. Make sure they understand the committee's charge and help them get comfortable with their responsibilities. Staff should outline clearly and respectfully how the committee has functioned and what the staff member's role has been. Offer to support the chairperson as they assume leadership of the committee.

Then, staff uses their leverage — the agenda. Since the chair will control the meetings, it is critical that the assigned staff person help draft the agendas. This is not only proper, it is essential. And as I indicated earlier, well-planned agendas, which adhere to the goals of the committee, will make the chair a hero to his committee members and bond the chair/staff working relationship.

The agenda also keeps a rogue chairperson from running amok. Of course, if you have someone running a committee who forces their own agenda without regard to the charge, you have a problem. If this happens, staff should use all of their skill to persuade the chair to conduct balanced meetings and adhere to the committee's basic charge. If that doesn't work, then you as CEO may have to intervene, first to counsel your staff to create their own solutions, or eventually to speak directly to the chair.

The key then to facilitating committees is a harmonious and mutually respectful working relationship between staff and chair. Together they forge the committee's future, reflected in well-crafted agendas and good follow-through. From that foundation, committee work can be more easily accomplished, and the staff will already have greased the skids for ensuring the facilitation of resultant activities.

**4) Volunteer Training:** Volunteer training? Who needs it? Didn't we spend all of that time and effort recruiting expertise, experience and clout? Besides it costs money, no one will come anyway and my president says we don't need it, whatever it is.

Of course I'm joking. Even if you have heard such inane reasoning, as CEO you know that uninformed volunteers don't perform as well. At the board level, lack of training and knowledge can be potentially disastrous.

But once again, development of our volunteers often becomes a low priority. It is very easy to just not get around to it. First, the volunteers themselves aren't usually clamoring for it. More meetings is the last thing they will suggest. Let me clue you though, they may not ask for it, but they'll look to you if a time comes when they feel untrained in some element of organization business. Then again, they often don't know what they don't know. As effective professionals in their own field, they feel quite comfortable in fulfilling their responsibilities at the not-for-profit level. They assume business savvy is business savvy. It ain't. Take budgets for example. Most NFPs use fund accounting, most businesses do not. It may take a veteran banker some time before they really understand NFP accounting. They may keep trying to force your way into their way.

Volunteer development is another important element in your role as chief facilitator. It can also be a very trying and frequently delicate undertaking. Top flight professionals may not understand why they need training to be a volunteer. They may even resent the implication. But it has to be done. Start with your board. Today the legal issues facing NFP boards are increasingly complex. In every community across this country, it is not uncommon to see the mistakes of a NFP board showing up on the front pages of local newspapers. Frequently the issues revolve around fiscal management, conflict of interest, board/staff blowups and so on. On examination, the reason for these mistakes has often been sloppy work by the board of directors. The specter of such possibilities should be sobering to any board, and every CEO. Who do you think the board will look to first when it comes to laying blame?

Theoretically every board should demand training which focuses on their legal and ethical responsibilities and risks. Some do, most don't. Should they? Yes. Quite honestly, I think they may be aware of the risks, but like a car wreck, the problems will happen to some other board; not to your board with all of the nice people on it. So whose responsibility is it to see that your board is properly informed? In theory the board itself should see that its members receive appropriate training. They are the legally responsible governing body of the organization.

What really happens is either nothing, or the CEO steps in. You should step in as the administrative steward of your organization and facilitate the training of all volunteers, not just the board. In fact, volunteer training should be in your annual budget. The volunteers will respond if training is offered. Down inside, they know they need it. They will even appreciate it.

So lead! Work with your president on a plan for board education. If he or she balks, toss a few reminders of fiduciary responsibility out on the table. That should get the proper attention. In fact, draft an annual program for volunteer training.

**The following are a few training opportunities you might consider:**

➤Mission and programs, every volunteer should be familiar with these important organizational elements,

➤Legal responsibilities of NFP Boards of Directors and NFP law,

➤Basic organizational orientation for new board members and other new volunteers,

➤The budget, make sure everyone on your board understands your budget and fiscal policies and that budget committee members are familiar with the type of accounting procedures used,

➤Financial development, especially for the board and its role in fund raising,

➤Consultants, use paid consultants to train or facilitate volunteers on specific subjects, *i.e.,* strategic planning, board self-assessment, fiscal control, human resources, planned giving, marketing, etc.

➤One-on-one, each volunteer should receive individual training and orientation when they join a committee or take on a specific project.

**5) Staff Training:** The logical tie-in to volunteer training, is to provide good staff training opportunities. As CEO you should take good care of your people. Budget as generously as you can for their continual development as professionals. The reasons are obvious:

➤It raises their self-esteem and sense of worth to the organization,

➤They increase their knowledge and enhance their skills,

➤They feel your personal support of them as individuals,

➤It serves as an incentive for good employees to stay with you,

➤You may unleash hidden abilities of a marginal employee,

➤A strong staff training commitment is also a good recruitment tool,

➤Gives increased evidence to the volunteers that they are working with and being facilitated by quality staff.

With the volunteers, you can balance between outside and in-house training. However, with staff, unless you manage a very large NFP, you will almost exclusively be sending your people off site. I encouraged my people to come to me with any training offering they might like to attend; this includes support staff as well. Together we assessed the value, application and cost of the offering. Usually, if the budget allowed, I supported their choice. I do suggest that you use a variety of training resources:

➤Your own organization's state, regional or national courses (if applicable),

➤Local or regional conferences, seminars, workshops offered by local consultants, colleges and universities; or selected traveling seminars,

➤University course work, usually local,

➤Networking conferences; sometimes ones you help organize,

➤Memberships in professional societies related directly to their field; such peer to peer contact is very reinforcing and positive.

**6) When to Shove:** Getting volunteers to live up to their implied agreements of responsibility isn't always easy. From time to time you may have to deal with volunteer procrastination, irresponsibility, or something as simple as having the right person in the wrong place.

First off, let's agree that in this business, volunteers work for us only after the priorities of their family and job. Then we get in the running with their other community work, hobbies, recreation, entertainment and personal time. So it isn't surprising that even our best volunteers sometimes have to miss a meeting or become an occasional no-show.

Usually volunteers who have agreed to work with you, do what is expected. But what should you do when they don't, when they drop the ball repeatedly? Tough call. The good news is, unless you've been recruiting poorly, or not spelling out expectations clearly, you only have to deal with this problem occasionally. The bad news is, you will have to remove a problem volunteer sometime, a duty which must be handled with care and diplomacy. But you shouldn't shy away from firing a volunteer when it's called for.

While each case of a recalcitrant volunteer is unique, there are some procedural steps you might want to consider:

➤Usually a staff member will come to you with news of a chronic no-show, an acerbic attitude problem, or similar difficulty. Discuss the problem with them and suggest a moderate course of action, *i.e.*, work through a chairperson, asking them to make a personal call. If it is the chairperson, the staff person should make a courtesy call and ask diplomatically if there is a problem they can help with. Soft sell, probing to see what's really going on. Often easily resolved at this point.

➤First effort doesn't work? Reassess the volunteer's motives and incentives. Perhaps they are just in the wrong slot and would respond favorably to a new assignment. If that isn't the problem, repeat first step. The person in question may then offer to resign or be more forthcoming about the reasons for their unacceptable performance.

➤Second inquiry fails? The CEO meets with the staff member again and reviews the details and steps taken to date. If the volunteer in question is a chairperson, a letter of supportive inquiry should go out from another chair in a superior post, or the board president. If the person is not a chairperson, the chair of the committee should either try to call again or send a letter of supportive inquiry.

➤By this point, most volunteers receiving this kind of attention will have responded and either cleared up a misunderstanding and returned to duty, or apologized and resigned. Then you're left with the miniscule number of irresponsible or clearly unavailable people.

➤Do not waste a lot of additional time. You, your staff, specific chairs or the president have done your best. A letter relieving them of their position, written kindly, must go out. Finis.

➤One reminder, don't forget the triad during this process.

If a member of the board is involved, such as not attending board meetings, this should be easily cleared up with your board attendance policy in the bylaws. Of course, prior to implementing a policy of automatic dismissal after missing X number of meetings, all efforts should be made to give the person adequate notice. Remember, board members are often very unwilling to drop a fellow volunteer from their ranks. At the same time, they may also resent this person's absenteeism. Whatever the case, after the protocol of the matter has been administered, no attempts should be made to save dead wood.

As CEO you should communicate with your president regarding the absentee board member, but leave the action to the board. You may point out a chronic attendance problem and suggest its effect on the board's ability to govern, but stay out of the way. Do not risk your board's disapproval, which would happen if you're seen as meddling in their affairs too deeply.

**Note:** If your bylaws do not have a board member attendance clause, they should.

**7) Rewards:** Regardless of what people say about plaques and other awards, I've never seen anyone turn them down. Even the gaudiest gewgaw trophy still says, "Hey, you're pretty special". And when such an award or some other recognition comes from a group of one's peers, it is even more special.

Never pass up the opportunity to say thanks. It doesn't always have to be a plaque, and in most cases it isn't when it's among you and your volunteers. The key to rewarding your people is keeping good records: the committees they've served on, chairmanships they've held, board terms, offices they have held, special achievements, years of service and so forth.

Someone a few years ago coined the term *psychic income*. I've used it ever since to define the benefits of volunteer service; the nonmonetary pay back for giving of yourself to a cause. Part of it, to be sure, is the self-satisfaction one gets from doing something worthwhile. But the rest of it is the *visible and spoken* appreciation received for their efforts. Rewarding volunteers is really an ongoing, daily function of the staff and the volunteers themselves.

**Here are examples of direct and indirect ways to reward:**

➤**The Spectacle:** Most NFPOs have annual awards functions of some kind. Usually it is a luncheon or dinner devoted entirely to saying thanks in a very public way. There are lots of words, trophies, plaques and certificates. Most importantly, those who are deserving are recognized in front of their peer group.

➤**Letters:** Getting a letter from someone expressing appreciation for a job well done is always a winner: from the CEO, the president, the chairperson or a staff member.

➤**A Note from You:** A hand written note from the administrator is something no one else can do. It is always in order. Never underestimate the respect your position holds in the organization.

➤ **Newsletter:** Feature someone in your organizational newsletter; use their picture whenever possible — a real plus.

➤ **Spoken:** Give a public word of appreciation or congratulations on someone's behalf at a board or committee meeting, or just make a phone call to say thanks.

➤ **CEO's Report:** Include words of commendation about someone in your monthly report.

I'm sure you can add to this list. You can never say thanks or reward volunteer (and staff) achievement too often. Rewarding your people is the end result of doing a good job of facilitating their efforts.

# RECAP

Never forget that the volunteers came first, well before they hired a CEO. It should keep you humble to remember that. It is your job to remind your staff that first and foremost, they are to use their professional skills to facilitate volunteer achievement.

They should view a volunteer's time as a donation and spend it wisely. Committees drive NFPs, like it or not, and agendas drive committees. An agenda is a formal agreement, a covenant to perform, a promise to be lived up to. As CEO, you must focus on facilitating the board process. To do that you'd better be in close contact with your president. Keep the board concentrating on the organization's mission — its purpose for existence. The same goes for your staff and its relationship with the committees. They must respect your committees, the chairs and the agreements to use volunteer time and talent wisely. You have an obligation to train your volunteers, it is simply good business to do so. The same goes for staff. Know when to shove reluctant volunteers, or even fire them, as well as when to reward those who excel. Finally, you can never say "thank you" too often.

# CHECKPOINT FOUR

# Dollars In, Dollars Out

So far we've been dealing with matters wherein the CEO is more or less free to develop his or her own style, if done with integrity and diplomacy. Now we're entering the arena where everyone plays, where everyone has an opinion. *This is the budget*; land of CPAs, auditors, the IRS, Better Business Bureaus, attorneys general, investment managers, budget committees and boards of directors. We are talking numbers. You know what numbers do? They always add up the same. They are exact. Everybody uses them in a similar manner. And everybody thinks they know what your numbers are saying. People love to pour over numbers.

Forget charisma and professional style if your numbers don't jive. Many good NFP CEOs have been handed their walking papers over bad numbers. Bad numbers make boards look bad. Bad numbers flash in neon and draw lots of attention. Boards don't want to look bad.

Here's my advice about numbers. Got your high-lighter? *Never handle the numbers alone.* Back in Checkpoint One, under Managing a De-

*Notes*

mocracy, I spoke of a triad. Here's another one. When it comes to your budget, cash in, cash out, share it with a triad. This time it's the budget committee, your controller, and the board. Never lead with your chin when it comes to managing the financial resources of your NFPO. I don't care if you were a CPA in your former life, don't fool around with the numbers like the Lone Ranger.

It's not a question of how adept you are at reading a balance sheet. What we're talking about here is public accountability for money people gave your tax exempt organization. The government, the watchdog groups, and your donors will not look kindly on you if you get sloppy with donated money. Some NFP CEOs mistakenly try to always make the numbers look good for the board, even when they aren't; or having only cursory budget sessions once or twice a year — unacceptable. Since you won't operate that way, let's look at some of the things you will do:

**1) Budget Committee:** Call it what you want, finance committee, budget committee, finance and audit committee, whatever you like

— just have one. Rule one, recruit the best committee of financially astute people you can find. Don't settle for somebody's uncle who has a great head for numbers. May work, may not. It's not worth the risk. You want certified expertise and a credible image. Brand names.

Actually, recruiting a strong budget committee can be one of the easier tasks facing you. First, we're being very focused here — finance. Secondly, the woods are full of people who count, hold and manage other people's money. There is usually a generous supply of that type of talent available. Also in many cases, the banks, CPA firms and other businesses are among those companies which encourage community service. Many professional careers are even enhanced because of demonstrating active civic leadership.

Look at the large and medium sized CPA firms, the banks, insurance corporations and seasoned business managers of respected companies. Your budget committee should be large enough to allow for a few no-shows each meeting. Accountants and bankers often get tied up with clients at a moment's notice. The budget committee should meet monthly. That's right, monthly. In my opinion, once a quarter isn't adequate. Keep on top of this responsibility. The budget committee profile might look like this:

➤CPAs — at least two, no more than three (Price Waterhouse, Peat Marwick types, and well known regional firms); veterans, not junior accountants

➤Bankers — one or two, try the vice president corporate level (branch managers may be less flexible with their time)

➤Investment Manager — find a corporate level vice president who manages company investments. (This person will be critical to help monitor your investment funds manager, if you have retained one). It may be best to not recruit an investment manager who oversees other NFP portfolios on a client basis; this may lead to conflict of interest problems. Nor should you retain an investment manager who sits on your budget committee or your board of directors

➤Business Executive — locate a respected hands-on business executive of a well known company

➤Corporate Controller — the controller of a good-sized company would also be a good addition

➤You should probably have a budget committee comprised of around seven or eight members total, reflecting a balance of the disciplines mentioned.

This committee should receive complete, accurate reports, that are well prepared. By all means give them everything — the full, unvarnished data. You must have their trust or they will become your severest critic, as they should if you are providing less than full disclosure or are consistently unprepared. You want them to be a full partner in the budget triad.

**2) The Controller:** This member of the triad, you hire. Choose this person carefully. There is usually a good selection of available accounting talent, so take your time. Depending on the size of your organization, pay all you can justify for your in-house accountant. If you're on the small side and can only afford a bookkeeper, get a good one. Do your homework, check references on this one all the way. You may want to have a couple of members of your budget committee help screen applicant resumes for you. In fact, I recommend it. Their professional insights will be of great assistance and their sense of participation means they are buying into your eventual selection. However, the final selection should be yours.

If you are large enough to afford a true director of finance and budget, do it. You don't need a CPA necessarily. There are usually many talented accountants, from private companies and other sources available. Select a controller who will work with you, who can see the jar as half full, not half empty. Some accountants are stuck in a rut, the rut of what you can't do. Make sure that you pick someone who will find a way to reflect financial data in the most favorable light for your organization. I'm not saying to cut corners or be unethical, just keep the organization's best interests in mind. There are usually many ways to say the same thing. Your controller should use approved accounting principles to tell your story well.

Your controller should also turn out top quality financial reports which meet the approval of your budget committee. Committee members should be able to easily interpret the data and answer inquiries effectively at committee or board meetings. In addition, if you've got a real gem, the controller should do the research and make recommendations on capital purchases, insurance plans, employee benefits, and other technical matters where you need accurate analyses upon which to base intelligent decisions.

**3) The Audit:** I'm surprised when I hear of a NFP which doesn't conduct an annual audit. Most nationally based or large NFPOs require that an outside audit be done every year by a qualified CPA. Some misguided organizations don't get around to it for one reason or another. I suspect those which don't are in the minority. Every NFPO should have a formal audit every year. Your budget committee should help select an auditor who has experience in NFP fund accounting. In the beginning, you should look at three or more firms. Firms represented on your budget committee, board or other committees, should not be considered normally due to conflict of interest. Do not take that lightly. More and more funders, as well as the Better Business Bureau and other surveillance groups, expect every NFP to have a policy on conflict of interest. Point: No board director, officer or other volunteer should benefit personally through their participation in the affairs of the NFP. No personal gain, period. No appearance of personal gain, period.

Ask the CPA firms interviewed to submit a bona fide bid to conduct your audit. Balance cost with the level of confidence you have in each candidate. Once an audit firm has been selected with the assistance of your budget committee (I suggest you go with the firm they prefer unless you have good reason not to), ask them for a list of in-house duties your controller can perform in advance of the audit to help reduce their fee. Usually they will provide such a list and it can bring down your costs substantially. In fact, most auditors really prefer it if much of the minutiae has been taken care of by your staff, even if it does lower their fee. They are more efficient if basic bookkeeping and documentation level work has been done.

Also request a formal management letter. When your audit is completed and you have received the management letter, the budget committee chair should invite the auditor to meet with the committee to review his or her findings. Remember, when you ask an auditor to prepare a management letter, which they must later defend, they will usually suggest some improvements to be made in your accounting procedures; that's just the nature of the process. Still and all, it is an exercise worth doing. First, you can always produce the management letter to prove you've been practicing prudent financial review. Secondly, you may actually receive some suggestions which will improve your fiscal procedures and even save you money on the next audit.

You'll probably want to stay with an audit firm for a number of years. The pluses are that they know your NFP, you gain confidence in them, you can stabilize costs and your budget committee keeps them on their toes. Every three to five years, you might want to consider other firms just so neither side gets complacent. I suggest you change only if you've lost confidence in your auditor, costs escalate beyond reason or there have been serious errors of some type. Except for very large NFPs, you may be best served by contracting with a small to medium-sized CPA firm. In most cases you will get a senior or very experienced auditor; perhaps even a partner.

If you go to one of the majors, your NFP will likely be assigned to junior staff who will cut their teeth on your account. NFP accounting is unique enough that you should only have accountants experienced in NFP audits doing your work, if at all possible. Besides, junior staff in a large firm may actually cost you more because it takes them longer to do the work. If they need senior staff assistance, those billable hours will run very high. This doesn't mean you should exclude the major CPA firms out of hand. Just be assured that they will assign you staff with NFP experience at a fair price.

**4) Investment Portfolio:** If your NFP is large enough to place a portion of its funds in an investment position, don't be casual. It is usually best to secure an investment manager, again selected by your budget committee. Remember that an investment expert should sit on your budget committee. This is where they can do their stuff as monitor of the investment manager's performance. Most firms will not take on your funds to manage separately if they are not significant enough to warrant their time. Your investment expert can probably advise you and the budget committee on this. If your available funds are not enough to attract a qualified investment manager, there are a number of pooled investment fund opportunities you can look into. Always seek and use qualified professionals to advise you and your committee in this area.

Whether free standing portfolio, or pooled fund, you should have investment guidelines. Such guidelines tell your fund managers under which parameters they may invest your NFP's funds. Your guidelines should be clear, professionally drawn and give your manager as much freedom as possible without violating the level of risk agreed to by your organization. Having such investment guidelines is a good business practice and reflects prudence on behalf of the organization and its board. The guidelines must be approved by the board before being enacted.

I heartily advise against the budget committee, or separate volunteer investment committee, serving as the organization's investment managers. First, the committee will only meet monthly under ordinary circumstances, reacting to market conditions which change daily; even hourly. In addition, it may open the organization to possible criticism for handling such a trust less prudently than it should. The key here is to seek professional counsel on investing NFP funds, no matter which methods are eventually selected.

**5) Insurance:** Today, one of the top two or three questions a CEO may be asked by a prospective NFP board member is, "Do you carry board liability insurance?". It is a sign of the times. When was the last time you checked your *exposure coverage*? Exposure coverage is insurance which protects the organization, its directors, officers and CEO from threat of liability related to organization functions. Every NFPO should carry adequate insurance for this purpose. You should seek professional advice to determine which and what levels of various liability and bonding coverage your organization should be carrying. As the inherent risks frequently change in scope, you should review your exposure coverage at least annually. And of course, select an insurance broker carefully. Establish a relationship of confidence and an understanding by them of your unique needs. In many cases, if you are affiliated with a national organization, much of your insurance may be purchased on a co-op basis. I would even compare those figures locally, however. Sometimes you can beat the national rates; though that is not usually the case.

**Some of the types of insurance in this category may include the following:**

➤Director's and officer's insurance
➤General liability
➤Umbrella liability

➤Medical expense

➤Non-owned and hired auto liability

➤Fidelity bonding insurance (covers employee dishonesty)

➤Travel accident

➤Incidental malpractice liability

The above list is for your information only and is not intended to be all inclusive. Seek competent professional advice, but do not leave your organization without adequate coverage.

**6) Dollars Out:** Your budget is set. The fiscal year begins. You start spending money. You have twelve months to go — the dollars need to reach. Your board expects you to spend wisely and within the established budget. Here is where your budget committee really shines. Every month you meet with them to review the crisp, informative financial reports prepared by your controller. They hash over any discrepancies, make appropriate adjustments, ask you and the controller pointed questions, then accept the data as presented if they are satisfied. At your next board meeting, the budget committee chair presents a financial report to the directors, volunteer to volunteer. The triad works again. There is confidence in the data — all is well with the world.

In between times, your controller comes to you with questions or suggestions which keep the budget on track, or points out problem areas. You confer, course corrections are made before the next budget meeting and so it goes. The numbers are all out in the open, being massaged and lined up by the controller, scrutinized by the volunteer experts and endorsed by the board. Ah, the triad, savior of CEOs.

**7) Dollars In:** Spending is comparatively easy, as long as you stay within the lines. Bringing dollars in is a different story. There's no magic formula. Outside of a very few fund raising geniuses, it's just plain hard work, head to head competition; and it requires study and skill. But we all know that as a CEO today, you are expected to play a significant role in attracting funds.

The biggest demand on NFP CEOs is not what programs to implement. The demand on CEOs today is where to find the funds. No funds, no program. To survive as a CEO you had better have a fund raising game plan. But like everything else, don't try to do it alone. As CEO, you are the orchestra leader. You can't possibly play every instrument, and people will resent, even judge you if you try. Ownership. Everything I've been saying so far is about ownership. It should be no different for financial development.

Don't let your board off of the hook on development. Provision of resources is a primary function of NFP boards. That fact has to be revisited with them regularly. Advising your board that they need to get behind program is relatively easy, compared to reminding them of their responsibilities for funding. It can be a delicate matter. You must do it however.

Before reminding them, make sure you have several things in order. You need a staff member assigned to development. If you are a small NFP, that could be you; probably should be. If you're lucky, you have a staff development director. Then of course you need a development committee. See what we're developing — another triad.

Next, you need a strategic plan for development. You, your development director and development chair should hammer that out. Once the committee and staff have fleshed it out and fine-tuned it, take the plan to the board. That plan should include board responsibilities. Your development chair should have been selected because he or she is dynamic and fearless. That person should also be a board member and will be the one to present the strategic development plan to the board. Their job: Get the board's endorsement and commitment.

Once you have the development plan in place, it has to be implemented. That's where the rubber meets the road. At year's end, everyone will still be looking for the bucks, no matter who accepted ownership of the plan. Backing up the plan should be good development staff, sound funding mechanisms, effective use of resources and the influence of your volunteers, especially those with clout. In every case, it's nice to have the triad out there, but results are still expected. No where are the expectations more profound than in raising dollars. So when prioritizing your time, I suggest that development be at or very near the top.

---

# RECAP

Your style and charisma won't count for much when it comes to managing your organization's money. The bottom line is always the bottom line. Make sure the numbers balance. Hire the best controller you can afford, recruit a top notch budget committee and turn out succinct, accurate financial records for the board. Always conduct an annual audit, performed by an outside firm, and request a management letter from your auditor. If you have funds to invest, set sound investment guidelines and use a professional investment manager. You protect all of this activity by carrying adequate liability and bonding insurance for board officers and directors, the CEO and staff. Finally, spend wisely and raise lots of money. On the sixth day walk on water and remember, never handle the money alone.

**NOTE:** There are many reference books available on accounting, including a variety aimed at specific NFP disciplines. I suggest you talk with your auditor, or members of your budget committee who are CPAs, and ask them to recommend specific texts to you. One volume which is among the best for your controller to review is:

*Standards of Accounting & Financial Reporting for Voluntary Health & Welfare Organizations;* Published by: National Health Council, Inc.; National Assembly of Voluntary Health & Social Welfare Organizations, Inc.; United Way of America.

# CHECKPOINT FIVE

# Out and About

While budgets, recruitment and managing your NFP democracy demand ever vigilant attention, don't do it in a vacuum. As the saying goes, what goes around comes around. As CEO your ability to recruit good people, raise money and all of the rest is dependent on knowing and being known.

So get out of your chair, your office and your own cloistered environment. The community that supports your organization should also be served by you. You can't just ask, ask, ask. You need to invest of yourself and your organization over time. Even if you were so insensitive as to expect to join a local civic organization one day and expect a contribution for your NFPO the next, it doesn't work that way. Just as *you* would spot insincerity in a minute, so to would your intentions be recognized.

Be the same high quality, respected volunteer you seek for your own organization. Serving on boards and committees is a vital experience for any NFP CEO.

*notes*

It is a constant reminder of how it feels to be a volunteer. You will experience the same sense of vulnerability, frustration and satisfaction as those who volunteer for you. And you should be one heck of a volunteer; a dynamite chairperson or terrific committee member — focused, dependable, positive and effective. If *you* don't offer those traits who will?

# What to Join and Why

Of course you can join so many community groups that you hurt your own performance back at the ranch. It is easy to become a *joining groupie.* Just as you wrinkle your brow over a prospective volunteer who already belongs to 14 other organizations, your own effectiveness is reduced by such a practice. Join, but be selective and limit the number of assignments you take on. Pick opportunities which cover the bases, but are also of personal benefit to you as well. Nothing can be gained from getting involved with a cause or group of people if that involvement is drudgery or you resent the time spent and perhaps don't even enjoy the people. It is okay, even required to say no to invitations which will not be good for you or useful to your NFPO. That is not to say that every group you decide to join will offer you only mountain top experiences. I'm sure you wouldn't even expect such luxury. You should expect to expend effort and offer commitment, of course — but not at the cost of personal satisfaction and it should be for a credible purpose. Anticipate the same rewards you offer your own volunteers. However, mostly you will join outside organizations for business purposes.

**Here is a list of the basic reasons why a NFP CEO should get out and about:**

➤**Representation:** Your NFPO should be represented with a variety of organizations for reasons important to your mission. In a select number of those instances, the CEO should be the one who is representing your organization.

➤**Experience:** To lead and facilitate your NFPO, it is important for you to continually gain new experiences serving on boards and committees yourself.

➤**Command Performance:** In some cases, it is just expected that you will belong to certain groups, those closely affiliated with your cause — you know of those to which I refer.

➤**Simply to Be Seen:** In a very few instances, you may join an organization purely for the exposure it gives you and your NFPO. On those occasions, your absence would be more noticeable than your presence. Surely this is a weak reason but sometimes necessary.

➤**Resource Development:** Memberships offer the chance to develop acquaintanceships or relationships which may lead to future financial support for your NFPO. In financial development, the axiom is that *people give to people,* and usually to people *they know.*

➤**Contacts/Influence:** By joining selectively and putting in your time in the trenches, you will earn a valuable network of contacts, which may yield important influence when it is needed. A flash in the pan will never reap such benefits.

➤**Action:** Some memberships will help you and your NFPO reach some goal or create action beneficial to your cause. For example, joining or helping organize a coalition may bring about results which your NFPO could never have achieved alone.

➤**Professional Development:** There are obvious benefits from maintaining memberships in professional societies and associations. Keeping up on the latest developments in your field and networking with your peers, these are essential activities.

➤**Personal Benefit:** Don't forget your own personal interests. On occasion you will join an organization for your own enjoyment *and* the mutual benefit of your organization. Remember, recruiting, developing contacts, resource development — all of these and more can come from groups which may seem totally unrelated to your NFPO's purpose.

## Choose Wisely

I firmly believe that every professional staff member should belong to organizations which can extend the reach of their NFPO. As CEO you should consider such affiliations for your staff. Use good judgement when determining the most effective use of your staff for this purpose. Again, do not overextend your people anymore that you would yourself, but encourage them to become involved outside of your organization as well. Make sure the right people assume the right affiliations. Never waste a CEO level membership on someone else. Nor should the CEO fill a position more suited for a staff member. But for now, let's concentrate on where you as CEO should spend your membership tokens in the community.

You may or may not already belong to a number of organizations. In either case, let's look at the spectrum of these opportunities. It may be time to review your memberships, and certainly if you are totally isolated in your office, let's get you out of there. Perhaps you don't consider yourself a joiner and look upon those of your peers who do as glory seekers and busy bodies. Granted some may deserve such criticism, but most do not. It is quite simply, part of your job. Whether eager or reluctant, well selected affiliations will only add to your prestige with your board, staff, and volunteers — as well as the community at large.

Obviously in any community, the number of organizations to which you could belong may seem endless. And in each place there will be organizations which are unique. It is up to you to assess your own community, judge the strengths and weaknesses of select organizations and make your own intelligent choices.

**Here are a few classifications which you should consider:**

➤ **Civic Clubs:** Expect weekly time commitments, high expectation of involvement, very social environment, and a varying degree of influential members. Do some checking on which clubs are thought of most highly in your community and will meet most of your expectations. Some civic clubs require an invitation to join. However, such clubs are always looking to build membership. It should be relatively easy find someone to sponsor you. Long term commitment here should yield contacts, networking resources, potential volunteers and friendships. A few examples of civic clubs includes: Rotary, Kiwanis, Lions, Civitan, Active 20-30, Jaycees and Optimist. All civic clubs have special projects which they sponsor to benefit their communities. They expect their members to support those projects with time and money. Due to the time commitment, you should consider only one civic club membership. In fact, most civic clubs frown on dual memberships anyway.

➤ **Chambers of Commerce:** The chamber offers the opportunity to be in contact with many of your community's business leaders. Again, the payoff will be through committing yourself to work effectively at the committee level. Frankly, chamber boards in most metropolitan areas are reserved for major business owners and top echelon business CEOs. However chambers are more attuned to expanded representation than they used to be.

Multicultural and women members are now regularly elected to chamber boards, from a variety of business backgrounds. If your NFPO fills a special niche, you could be invited to sit on the chamber board. This would be an exception however, unless you are in a smaller community where your status might carry more weight. The chamber board is after all supposed to represent business. Since NFPOs don't meet the for-profit profile in the commercial sense, to them you aren't considered technically in business. Of course we know that you are in business. You must manage your organization like a business: generate revenue, meet payroll, compete in the marketplace, pay the rent, deliver services, stay on budget and make a profit. Except in your case, the profit is not paid out to shareholders or board directors.

But this subtle argument may not gain you a position on the traditional chamber board. So seek instead membership on any of a number chamber committees. Just like any other organization, your chamber of commerce needs its members to volunteer for committee work. Pick an area of interest you might enjoy, have expertise in or see as a way to rub shoulders with a specific element of the business community. Then dig in, be an effective volunteer and wait for positive results — contacts, chairmanships, candidates for your own board and so forth.

➤**Government Advisory Committees:** Most branches of local government, city, county and state, use a variety of citizen advisory committees. These committees seek community input from consumers and expertise from providers of specific services. Members are appointed by the administrative heads of various agencies or elected officials. Public agencies usually issue a call of some sort for candidates to serve on advisory committees. Frequently groups and organizations which have a purpose closely related to a specific agency will receive a written request for suggested candidates to serve on a board, task force or committee. Frankly, some of these committees can be a frustrating waste of time; others will be more suitable for selected members of your staff; still others, a good investment of your time. As with any membership you may consider, do your homework.

**In my opinion, government advisory committees must offer several of the following opportunities to the CEO to be taken seriously:**

**a) Contact with agency administrators:** If for no other reason, the opportunity to get to know certain administrators of government agencies or departments personally is often worth accepting appointment to an advisory committee.

**b) Effect change:** Government advisory committees may provide significant input on matters of budget, program and long term goals. If the committee offers credible opinions and suggestions, officials will give that input serious consideration. And if you and your peers on the committee bring respected expertise and credentials to the table, even more impact may occur. Public agencies are often required to have advisory committees and must give their input credence. Hopefully, the agency will be targeting an area of importance to your NFPO.

**c) Networking:** With each membership you accept should come an opportunity to network with a different professional or business segment of the community. There may be some overlap, but usually chamber of commerce members will differ from those on the county human services advisory board. Instead of business owners and CEOs, on government advisory committees you'll usually sit with social workers, university professors, health care professionals, engineers, transportation specialists or urban planners.

**d) Lead Time:** As a NFP CEO, you need to have your ear to the ground. Participating on citizen advisory boards offers you a pipeline to governmental developments which may impact your organization's goals. Many times, to learn of impending strategies, or even be a participant in designing them, offers you time to prepare; to be ready to respond with your own resultant actions. You're not gaining insider information, but you are involved firsthand and may gain that critical edge.

➤**Higher Education:** How many colleges or universities do you have in your community? Count them up. Considering state universities, private colleges and community colleges, probably more than you thought. Each one of those schools could potentially offer you several valuable avenues of affiliation. Like the government agencies, most institutions of higher education maintain advisory committees or boards, not counting the high powered boards of trustees and state boards of higher education. Every university department might have an advisory group made up of expertise from the community. What is your particular area of expertise? Have you ever been asked to speak to college classes as a community resource person? If so, that may be an open door to approach the department head to see if they have an advisory committee and offer your services.

Every college or university needs strong links with the community to gain expert advice and leadership, spokespersons, funding, enhanced reputation, influence and a sense of belonging to the community — just like your NFPO. In the past, universities often exuded an aura of arrogance which is no longer accepted. The need for more resources and credibility is bringing the towers of learning out into the community. They need you and you will benefit from the affiliation as well.

➤**Coalitions:** Earlier I mentioned *coalitions* as a means of creating action. With most memberships or affiliations outside of your own organization, you assume the goals of the group you're joining. You may later help create change, but essentially you are agreeing to accept the objectives already in place. With coalitions, you either want to create an organization to achieve specific action, or join a coalition with objectives which are of paramount importance to your NFPO. Coalitions may range everywhere from a networking roundtable of peer CEOs to a group of organizations banding together to effect change.

**Caution.** Coalitions may breed strange bedfellows. Don't get so enamored with the agenda that you lose sight of the groups with which you are affiliating. If you want to join an existing coalition, give careful study both to the group's member organizations and the purpose under which it operates, including written objectives. Do not risk your personal reputation, or that of your NFPO, by joining the wrong group for the right reasons, which may be poorly defined. It will be a waste of time and could tarnish your image. The good news is that a coalition made up of quality organizations, with a well-defined mission can be extremely effective and often quite powerful.

➤ **Professional Societies:** It makes good sense to join organizations which are in business to support your profession. But even there, you should sort out the best from the rest. If your field is mental health, the arts, human services, education or whatever, you are already aware of the organizations which speak to you from that perspective. I will leave it to you to make prudent choices and join the most beneficial. But join. Keep up on your field!

➤**Then there are those professional groups which speak more generically:** The American Society of Association Executives, and its local chapters, the National Society of Fund Raising Executives, and a variety of options unique to local communities. Again, choose wisely, join wisely. Keeping in touch with your professional peers can be a vital lifeline.

➤**All the Rest:** As I said earlier, the number of organizations to which you can belong may seem endless. I have mentioned the most basic options up to this point; those which should receive strong consideration. But most communities are usually awash with more possibilities than you have time. Some are particular to your area of interest so you will want to assess them along with those already mentioned. I've made no attempt to be all inclusive, indeed that would be a futile effort. My main purpose is to stimulate your thinking as to the options and opportunities.

If you've been actively involved in the community for some time, maybe it is time to reassess and even develop a new strategy for your chosen affiliations. If you're new to all of this or have just never taken the time, you owe it to yourself and your NFPO to study the possibilities. Look to someone whose opinion you respect in this area to serve as a mentor; perhaps a board member who is active, a peer NFP CEO or a business professional — even a relative.

## RECAP

 To be an effective NFP CEO, in the broadest sense, you must move about effectively within the community as well as

your own organization. You need to join appropriate organizations selectively for the purposes of: reminding yourself what it is like to be a volunteer, gain new experience, to serve your community, to be well represented, earn contacts and influence, achieve desired action, develop resources, grow professionally, and sometimes just because it's expected of you. But you should choose wisely. There are more options than you can possibly engage. As a guideline you may want to choose from among these primary groups: 1) civic clubs; 2) chambers of commerce; 3) government agency advisory committees/ boards; 4) higher education advisory committees/boards; 5) coalitions; 6) others known to you. The bottom line is to fill out your CEO status and be visibly active in the community — but do it wisely.

# CHECKPOINT SIX

# Wide Angle Lens

So you have your democracy in hand, you've recruited well, the volunteers' talents are being maximized, the organization is in sound fiscal shape and you're a dynamic leader in the community. What's left? *The future.* Every organization chews up "todays" with an insatiable appetite. They devour resources whether you are ready or not. So you cannot afford to get comfortable with even a healthy status quo.

Your funding sources are never a given. Even the most secure base of donors can erode slowly or change overnight. The NFPO's mission will be in a dramatic or gradually evolving transition. Your competition won't be resting either. Volunteers and staff will move on and need replacement.

**Perhaps your most important role as CEO is to challenge your NFP to face the future.** This means that you first have to challenge yourself to be open to change. Are you too comfortable with the warm environment you've created? Is everything just hunky-dory? If so, you're already in trouble. Who else but you is going to jump start the future? Even if you have dynamic, forward thinking volunteers, if *you* aren't so inclined, nothing will happen. That is just reality.

So if you cannot see yourself as the visionary, or don't want to be, start planning now for down-sizing your organization over the next few years; or being asked to leave. It verges on unethical for any NFP CEO to ignore his or her responsibility to lead the organization into its own future successfully. Frankly, it can be the most enjoyable and exciting part of your job. So now that we've cleared the air on the subject, let's dig into the CEO's role as the "wide angle lens" of the NFPO.

## Be the Catalyst

As we've stated previously, busy volunteers and a staff with more than they can handle are not going to be nagging you for more to do. Their energies will be focused on what is in front of them. Only the CEO has the high ground vantage point to see the entire picture. **You signed on to lead. This is where you earn your salary.** You are going to start by teaching people that the organization will have to change, that in the future what they are doing today may not be as important, perhaps not even relevant or good enough to reach organizational goals and compete. Of course you must present the need for change not as a criticism, but as an exciting opportunity.

A catalyst, by definition, is a substance which *modifies* without being *consumed* in the process. **That's you**, and here are some of the key catalytic elements:

➤ **Be a Visionary:** Visionaries are often called fanciful dreamers, out of touch with reality. And they are. If that trait is seen as a liability, it shouldn't be. To be a visionary you have to break free of the current structure, to examine other possibilities. You must feel the exhilaration of stretching the mission of your organization beyond today's reality. As a visionary there are no limits, nothing is too anything. Let your imagination explore all of the possibilities. Send your imagination out on a "mental bungee cord", test the outer limits.

➤ **Research With Abandon:** Once you've agreed to loosen your mind, to say it's okay to think bigger, better and farther, then you become free to explore. You may know your organization; the technical and professional aspects of its mission. That is only the jumping off point. Now you must study an entirely new realm of information, perhaps seemingly unrelated: demographics, trends, national and world issues, advertising/marketing indicators, a wider array of journals, news sources and current literature in the NFP sector. Start a *future-file*. Stick everything in it that strikes your curiosity, seemingly pertinent or not. Don't limit yourself. Acquire books and journals which are on the leading edge of the future. Learn. Develop the vision! You will use it.

➤ **Plant the Seed:** Of course you can't keep all of this vision to yourself or it will never see the light of day. You need to introduce new ideas and future concepts to your staff and your volunteers. As CEO, you are the Johnny Apple Seed of your organization. Begin by planting the seeds of the future, introducing those things which might significantly impact your NFPO. But remember that it may take a year or two, or even more, for some concepts to take root. You should expect new ideas to run off of people's minds like water off plastic at first hearing. In the beginning you may notice little acceptance of your concepts, or feel that no one is open to new ideas; especially your ideas. More likely, people will not yet have fully absorbed your vision and cannot see the future possibilities as clearly as you do. Be patient. They will need time to catch up.

Suddenly one day you will begin to hear those same ideas coming back to you; some of the very same concepts you had planted a year or so before. Not all seeds that are planted actually sprout. Such may be the case with many of your strategies for the future. Test the waters expansively, offer as many innovative possibilities as feasible. I recommend that you use both verbal and written methods to introduce new ideas. First, gently educate and informally suggest new directions or strategies. As you gain feedback, select the most promising concepts and prepare written outlines to be shared with key volunteers and staff for consideration. If you are on target, you should expect to begin hearing these ideas regenerated at some future point. Then you begin to share ownership and facilitate those who are eager to run with the future. **One more point.** Not all of your ideas will be winners, some may even prove to be losers. Don't let that stop you. Plus, you aren't the only person who will have good ideas. In fact, you are in deep trouble if you haven't recruited people with creativity. But you are the primary person who can give support and authority to push ideas forward.

➤ **Stimulate Creativity:** Most businesses and organizations develop a culture which reflects the attitudes and personality of the boss. If you're pompous and stuffy, your organizational environment will be likewise. But if you are open, good humored and reward new ideas and risk taking, you will have a vibrant, exciting place to work. Stimulate the creativity in your volunteers and staff alike. Encourage people to take reasonable risks and even fail at times. Applaud new ideas and urge your people to test them out. Share your own ideas, be willing to be vulnerable yourself. Let it be known that your ideas are no more sacred than the next person's. Reward ideas.Not everyone acknowledges their own creativity, but it's there. Some people bubble with enthusiasm, others are more likely to sit on an idea for awhile and study it before reluctantly letting it come out. Find a way to nourish creativity no matter what route it takes.

Obviously you can't have everyone focusing only on creating new ideas to gain the boss's favor, but usually that is not the problem. The more normal course is to stay with the known, the familiar or to focus on a work load already too heavy. It may take exceptional energy to extract the creativity from your staff and volunteers, but you must do it. Stale programs will need new vitality. Your mission will require new methods to succeed. Is the creativity bubbling in your organization?

# Research & Development

Every NFPO should have a laboratory in which to test new ideas and concepts. Not many do. Too often a new program is conceived on paper and immediately put to work, only to struggle under the full brunt of expectation. Such a scenario can be born out of need, but frequently there has been no thought of testing the premise. As CEO, it is entirely appropriate, and I think essential, that you create an R&D annual budget. Set aside an amount appropriate to the size of your organization solely to explore and test new ideas. If you can't get all you want the first year, start small and prove the value of this concept. Have your own internal grant application process. You should personally manage this budget and award funds from it to those who can prepare a worthy concept. Worthy doesn't mean a project must succeed, or that it must not involve risk, just that it seems reasonable and looks to the future.

If you have never had an R&D budget before, it may take some convincing of your board or budget committee to get it passed. However, as CEO you should claim an R&D budget as an essential management tool. To drive the point home, perhaps you can point to a past program which failed needlessly because it wasn't adequately researched and tested before implementation. Of course not all R&D activities cost a lot, but they still need a haven in which to operate. The point is, create an environment in which to incubate and study new ideas. Those which succeed will be the future strength of your NFPO.

## Ownership

I am not suggesting that just because you are the CEO that you alone possess all of the vision, creativity and dynamism of your organization. At least I hope that isn't the case. Certainly you have recruited talented people with good self-esteem and creative minds. It's there, it is always there. The trick is to unleash it and use it well. If your staff doesn't get encouragement from you to think big and stretch, they won't. Why should they beat their heads on the wall for nothing?

So, you *are* the catalyst. You do see the big picture. You *are* the one to encourage and provide an atmosphere which nurtures creative thought and vision. But once you've opened the door and suggested a new future, start looking for ways to share ownership of this exciting process. Patience will be required. Acceptance of new vision takes time. Rejection will be part of it too. Not all ideas will be winners, but that's okay. Having a few losers makes the process seem more accessible to everyone. If one of the CEO's big ideas flops, they may feel more inclined to risk too. The most important job you will have is to nurture this delicate culture, to challenge people to risk and look to the future. They must join with you in seeing that planning for the future is part of their responsibility.

# RECAP

The most important role for the CEO may be challenging his or her NFPO to face the future. A comfortable status quo will be devoured by an organization and leave it unprepared to compete in the years ahead. The CEO sees the whole picture. He or she must be the catalyst for change. The CEO should be the stimulus for the NFPO's vision. To facilitate the organization he or she must open the doors to new ideas, stimulate creativity and nurture ownership of the process. The most important and practical tool in this instance is a research and development budget, providing a laboratory in which to encourage and test new ideas and help them to flourish or fail. Above all, share ownership with all who will join with you.

# CLOSING THOUGHTS

# Closing Thoughts

As an administrator in the NFP sector, you've chosen one of the most fascinating fields of endeavor. Oh sure, it is full of frustrations, often unrealistic expectations, and it is the least well understood sector of our society. Most Americans would be hard pressed to explain the voluntary sector of this country. And yet, no other country in the world comes close to the level of voluntarism by its citizens than is found in the United States.

And while it is true that many volunteers might have difficulty explaining the mission and programs of the very organizations they serve, that doesn't mean they don't care or even that the organizations are sloppy. Personally, I think American volunteers are so focused on doing something good, that they just don't want to become immersed in all of the particulars of management. They come from pressure-packed jobs, stressful personal lives, an increasingly complicated society, and they just want to do something clean and clear. They want to make a difference; just point them toward the job to be done and don't mess things up with details.

*notes*

This doesn't mean they don't have opinions or don't on occasion attempt to micro-manage. In fact, in today's era of voluntarism, Americans who volunteer have more definite opinions about what is important to them than at any time in our history. When it comes to choosing a cause to serve, they know the issues most important to them, what they want to see happen, and what role they want to play in that mission. But they have busy lives and do not have the time to bury themselves in every segment of an organization's operation. And yet they expect sound management and professional leadership.

That is why your job as the NFP CEO is so critical and calls upon a person who willingly and enthusiastically responds to all of the issues enunciated in this book. The volunteers who hire you will have high expectations of you. They will look to you to guide them and the organization professionally, dynamically and with sensitivity. They will look to you to keep them out of trouble, to make sure they and their fellow volunteers achieve the objectives important to them, manage staff, raise money and come in under budget.

Managing a NFPO is perhaps one of the most underestimated professions in our society. People appreciate the charitable and philanthropic services provided in their communities: they donate to them, volunteer for them and support them as an essential segment of society. However, except for those few volunteer leaders close to the flame, most do not appreciate or understand the skill and expertise it takes to effectively administer a NFPO. Professionals with extensive backgrounds in business and the management of people will often view the very organizations on whose boards they sit as peaceful little entities which require none of the acumen of the real business world.

I say that not to criticize, only to point out that it takes a person who is fully aware of the idiosyncrasies of this field to succeed in it. Still and all, for those who bring the necessary aptitude, or are willing to develop it, nothing is more challenging and rewarding. In no other sector can you bring together all of the key elements of a community to bear on issues critical to the well being of the public. In no other profession do you have the opportunity to assimilate freely a myriad of human and material resources to tackle matters of importance beyond the business and governmental sectors. This third sector speaks to the heart and soul of our country and allows everyone to help solve problems, create solutions, serve humanity and simply make a difference.

If you've chosen this field of endeavor, welcome. Our society needs men and women to lead our voluntary organizations, leaders who can manage a democracy and empower people to fulfill important missions. To lead the NFPO, you must be willing to assume full responsibility, while sharing your authority with others, managing effectively, being a visionary, and all the while understanding that the complexity of your job will go largely underestimated. And yet, it is probably the most rewarding field of management in America. Congratulations, best wishes and ... remember the TRIAD.

## About the Author

**George B. Wright** has over 26 years of experience in the not-for-profit sector. He has managed at every key staff position within 501(c)(3) philanthropic and charitable organizations, and served on a wide range of community boards and committees. His experience encompasses grassroots community organizations and major state and national associations. He has served from general staff to CEO. A native of Oregon, he served for nine years as the Executive Director of the American Lung Association of Oregon.

Mr. Wright is currently a Principal with C3 Strategies, a consulting firm which serves the not-for-profit sector. He focuses his practice on issues which help organizations and their CEOs establish and maintain effective and innovative methods of operation. Mr. Wright resides in Portland, Oregon with his wife Betsy Wright, who is Co-Principal with C3 Strategies.

**C3 Strategies**
3495 N.W. Thurman – Portland, OR 97210-1283

# About C3 Strategies

**At C3 Strategies we serve the Not-For-Profit (NFP) Sector,** including: •the NFP organizations which comprise the sector, •the corporations which interact with the NFPs, and •the government entities which have a symbiotic relationship with the NFP sector.

**C3 Strategies works within the triad** of these sectors to forge partnerships, excellence, commitment and solutions.

**What are your concerns?** Board development •Organization in transition •CEO burnout •Corporate relationships •Governmental relationships •Financial development •Volunteer recruitment and training •Staff development •Association Management •Stymied?

**At C3 Strategies our mission is** *Together We Strengthen Commitment.* It is the strength of commitment within a NFP organization that makes it all work. Maybe together we can help you strengthen your commitment. Send the form below to: C3 Strategies, 3495 NW Thurman, Portland, OR 97210-1283.

---

Yes, I've read *The Not-For-Profit CEO.* I would like to discuss how C3 Strategies might help our organization. Please contact me ☐ by phone, ☐ by mail.

Name: _____

Title: _____

Organization: _____

Mailing Address: Street: _____

City: _____ State: _____ Zip: _____

Bus. Phone: _____ Res. Phone: _____

---

*Notes*

# Notes

*Notes*